MW01234046

This Plan Book belongs to:

If found, contact me here:

Phone: _____

Email: _____

Address: _____

Dedicated To:

YOU!
You deserve a business that makes your soul sing.

Also dedicated to my husband Lee Collins who cheered me on through the entire process. To Liz Fulcher for inspiring me to put my systems into workbook form and to Kristen Joy who lovingly walked me through the digital book design and publishing process.

Copyright © 2017 Natalie Marie Collins

All rights reserved. No part of this book may be reproduced or transmitted in any form or by any means, including but not limited to information storage and retrieval systems, electronic, mechanical, photocopy, recording, etc. without written permission from the copyright holder. For permission requests, write to: info@natalie-mariecollins.com, subject line "Attention: Permissions Coordinator"

Published by:
Topanga Publishing
Atlanta, GA

Biz Plan Book 2017 ed. / Natalie Marie Collins
ISBN-13: 978-1537797755
ISBN-10: 1537797751

Cover and Interior Designed by: Natalie Marie Collins - NatalieMarieCollins.com

WARNING !!!

THIS Plan Book CREATES CHANGE

Three years ago I did a scary thing. When my corporate job ended I decided it was time to follow my dreams of being an online based entrepreneur. I had been learning from others how to do it, but it was still a huge struggle to figure out how it all worked. There were so many different formulas to follow, but none of them resonated with me. They didn't feed my creative side that was begging to come out.

I needed something that would help me bring my dreams to life in a fun, yet practical way. I wanted powerful, soul filling results.

I searched high and low, picking up tips and tricks along the way, then I took a step back to look at it all and realized I was sitting on huge life changing information. I just had to put it all together in the right order.

And that's exactly what I did with the Biz Plan Book.

This Biz Plan Book will guide you through discovering your dreams and how to make them happen. It's a life changing breath of fresh air.

It will help you break down what passions drive you forward, get clear on your business mission, what to do if you get stuck, how to get focused and most importantly, walk you step-by-step through turning your passions into actionable steps so you can have the business you've always dreamed of.

For a free 3-month business planning course, go to NatalieMarieCollins.com.

How To Use This Workbook + Planner

(aka Plan Book)

 Go through each page of the workbook section and answer the easy-to-follow guided questions.

 After you've put together your dreams and goals, break them down into actionable steps and put them in the planner portion of this book.

 Put deadlines on your goals. Give yourself enough realistic time to accomplish them to set yourself up for success.

 Theme your months and weeks for some serious focused attention.

 Review your goals + dreams at the end of each month and follow the guided questions.

 Aim to make this Plan Book dog-eared, marked-up, sticky-noted and deeply familiar. It's your companion and guide to making this your best biz year yet.

 Breathe, you can do this!

MY BIG WHY

Knowing what your BIG WHY is, is extremly important when it comes to your business and life. It's what drives you and keeps you going. Answer the questions below:

WHY are you doing (or working towards) this dream business that you're doing? _____
_____
_____

what drives you? _____
_____
_____

who benefits? And why? _____
_____

what does it feel like? _____
_____
_____

My Business Mission is:

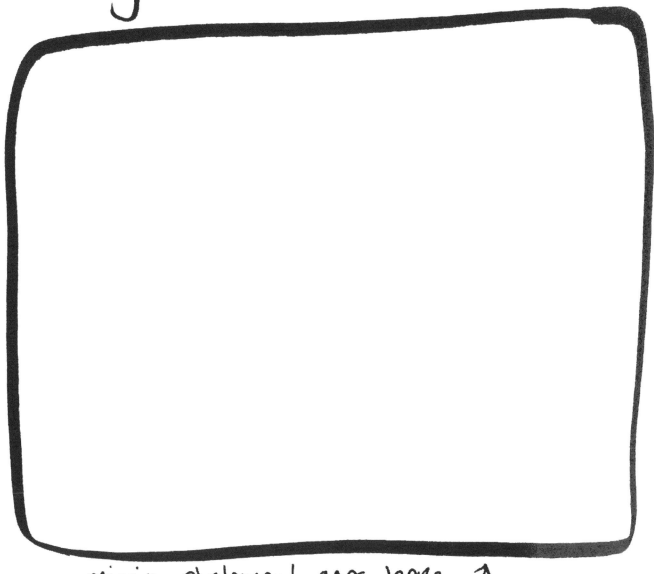

mission statement goes here ↗

Refer back to your business mission statement often. Especially during times when you might feel like you've gotten off your dream path. Use this to get yourself refocused on what's most important to you and your business. You can even cut it out and hang it up where you see it often.

If at anytime you feel

Stuck...

with filling out and going through these pages, do this:

Write With Markers!

Write, doodle, scribble, draw with markers to get the creative brain juices flowing.

Doodle down here

Create a Business Dream Board for 2017

Take images, cut them out or draw them below of what you want to bring into your business this year.

Dream BIG baby!

Intention Mandala

List 6 things, one for each petal, that you will strive to do daily to aid the Universe in bringing your dreams to you.

→ Suggestions: Prayer, Meditation, Writing, Walking/Exercise, Loving Gesture, Express Gratitude, Eat Healthy Foods, Sacred Space Time, Be Joyful, Random Act of Kindness

Are You Ready To Create Your DREAM BUSINESS?

Say YES!

Your mega ginormous dream PROGRAM (or service) of delicious brilliance you can't wait to share with the world goes here

Make It **BIG**!!! (like $1k++)

List everything you want to include in your Program:

Note: You can add more at any time. It's YOUR DREAM!

NOW
→ Circle 4 things in this box that you know TONS about + are super passionate about.

Next: Write down those [4] passion subjects in the boxes below: (1 per box)

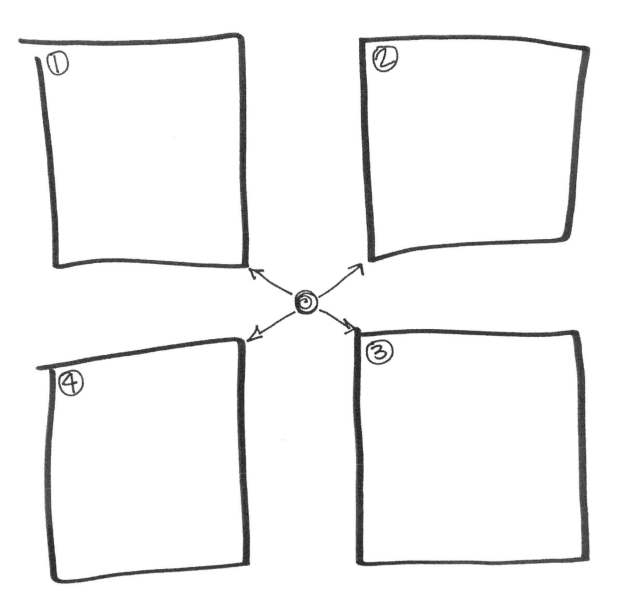

Each box represents 2 things:
① A part of your mega big course or service package that you are going to create into a stand-alone product.
② A quarter of a year.

If you are just starting out...

Take things slow and build on it. Rome wasn't built in a day and your business won't be either. Building a business takes time and dedication.

If you start out going too fast, you risk getting overwhelmed and burnt out. Nobody wants to get burnt out. It's not healthy for you or your business.

It's all about balance.

Start out by sharing just one piece of content with your tribe per week. Do this consistently every week and you will start to build your empire faster than you ever expected. Create the habit of once a week sharing, then as you get comfortable with one thing, add something else new to it that will enhance what you are already doing and repeat the process.

Get Started. Create the Habit. Build on it.

Business isn't a sprint, it's a marathon.

REMEMBER: You will also be building products/services in the background, so once a week sharing + product creating will keep you plenty busy in the beginning. You'll be learning new things, which usually takes longer than expected. Be gentle on yourself.

NOW... take all those topic commitments you just made and

Schedule it!

Write it all down in your calendar. Put a date on it! Commit to your success!

Tell yourself how serious you are about this and sign the Success Commitment Contract below:

Success Commitment

I, _____, solemnly swear to put my brilliant ideas, talents and gifts out into the world by committing to the business success schedule I have put in place.

I, _____, further swear to nurture and care for myself in the process.

Signed: _____
(your signature goes here)

Newsletters, Emails and Social Media... oh my!

Let's talk about sharing your content.

You've spent a lot of time + energy honing your gifts and putting all that brilliant content together, now it's time to share it with the world.

But how? Here are my two favorite ways:

→ Emailing your list
→ Social Media

There are probably a bazillion different formulas you could use in sharing your content. This is my favorite. Do what works best for you.

Create post → Share on social media → Send out monthly newsletter.

Write down your favorite ways to share your brilliance:

Don't Be Shy!

You have friends, followers and tribe members on your list...

WHY?

Because they love you + what you have to offer and want to know what you are up to. They want and need what you have. If you don't share it with them, you are robbing them of what they truly need...

YOU!

You have special talents and gifts that you were given for a reason. That reason isn't so you can keep them all to yourself. They are for you to share them with others.

So, share them already!

Each monthly layout has a newsletter planning section in the beginning. Use it to get serious about sharing. Be sure to schedule out when you are going to share your much needed gifts with others.

1st Quarter

The Passion Subject is: _____

→ Brainstorm all the different things you could share with others about this subject and add them to your idea bucket below.

... IDEAS ARE SAFE HERE ...

NEXT:

◎ Circle 3 things that meet these criteria :

→ Would make a great report, ebook, mini-course or some other kind of smaller product or service. ($97 or less)

→ People want to learn about it or receive it.

→ Is something you could create in 1-2 weeks.

1st Quarter's Focus: _____

(passion subject goes here)

→ In each box below, add 1 mini-product idea from the previous page. This is the product you will create for that month (before that month begins is best). This is also your theme for that month.

More on themes coming up.

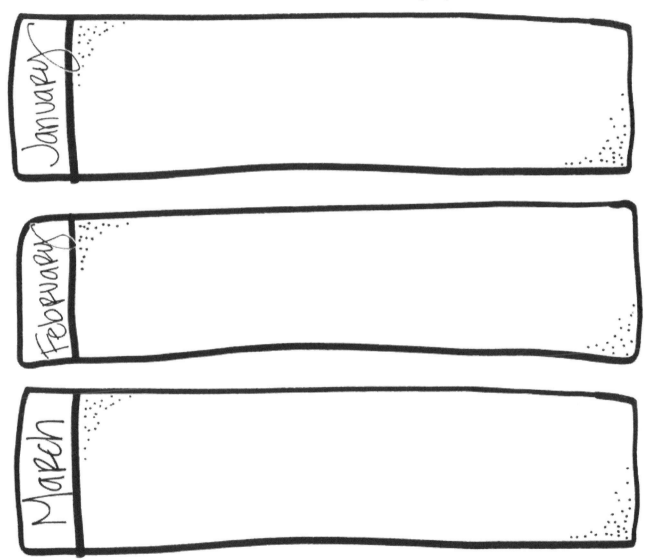

January

February

March

Each box is your sandbox of ideas to play in for that month.

NOTE: Creating your product the month before will increase your success.

Turn the page for more fun...

January's Idea Bucket

THEME: _____

(copied from sandbox)

→ **Brainstorm** all the different things you could talk/write/blog/video about this month's theme. Get specific. The more specific, the better.

Put your ideas in the bucket. Refer back to often for inspiration.

WEEKLY PLAN...

Lets talk FREE stuff, shall we...

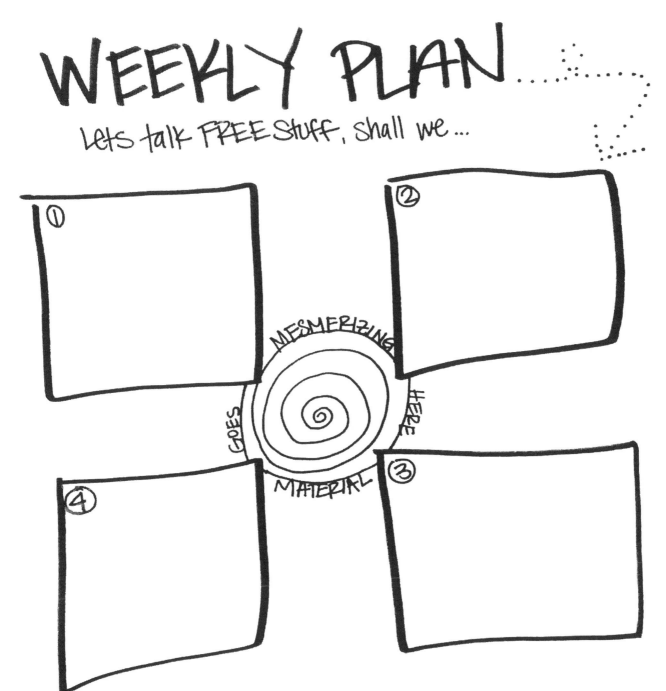

...Everyone loves free stuff. It's what attracts people to your business. In each box above, choose a topic of the week that revolves around your theme of the month. HINT: Check your idea bucket.

→Write down what you will do to share that content with others.

TIP: Free content are things like blog posts, infographics, lists, opt-ins, podcasts, videos, webinars, etc.

→Make the commitment and add them to your planner with due dates.

this month's January 2017

theme

reminders

goals

$

sunday	monday	tuesday
1	2	3
8	9	10
15	16	17
22	23	24
29	30	31

things to get done this month

newsletter(s)

mailing date(s):

topic:

related free content:

ways to generate buzz:

wednesday	thursday	friday	saturday
4	5	6	7
11	12	13	14
18	19	20	21
25	26	27	28

ideas | brainstorming | brilliance

January 2017

this week's focus	2 monday

good stuff	3 tuesday

	4 wednesday
"Comfort zones are for wimps." Rayven Perkins ColorMonthly.com	

email/newsletter/promo ideas

5 thursday		**to-do's**
		3 most important tasks
		☐ 1.
		☐ 2.
		☐ 3.

6 friday

7 saturday   **8** sunday

ideas | brainstorming | brilliance

January 2017

this week's focus	8 monday

good stuff	9 tuesday

"Everyone has a story worth telling and valuable knowledge to share—including you."

Candice L Davis
GoWriteSomething.com

10 wednesday

email/newsletter/promo ideas

11 thursday

12 friday

13 saturday

14 sunday

to-do's

3 most important tasks

1.
2.
3.

ideas | brainstorming | brilliance

January  2017

this week's focus | **9** monday

good stuff | **10** tuesday

11 wednesday

"A transformational journey to creating an extraordinary life starts by embracing your unique story. You are strong, brave, beautiful! You are an inspiration!"

Kristine Pierce
KristinePierce.com

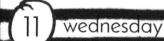 email/newsletter/promo ideas

12 thursday

to-do's

3 most important tasks

1.
2.
3.

13 friday

14 saturday   **15** sunday

ideas | brainstorming | brilliance

January 2017

16 monday

good stuff

17 tuesday

18 wednesday

"Coffee is
mandatory!"

Sherry Blair
WebsiteGrammaSherry.com

email/newsletter/promo ideas

19 thursday

to-do's

3 most important tasks

1.
2.
3.

20 friday

21 saturday

22 sunday

ideas | brainstorming | brilliance

January 2017

| this week's focus | 23 monday |

| good stuff | 24 tuesday |

| 25 wednesday |

"We are always looking out of our own eyeballs."

Rhonda Knight Boyle
RhondaBoyle.com

email/newsletter/promo ideas

26	thursday	to-do's
		3 most important tasks

1.

2.

3.

| 27 | friday |

| 28 | saturday | 29 | sunday |

ideas | brainstorming | brilliance

Monthly Checkin !

This is powerful stuff! ➔

"It is only in the review of your performance that you can have breakthroughs." -Steven Griffith

IMPORTANT: At the end of every month, take the time to reflect on how you felt about the past month, what you accomplished and what you feel you could improve on in the upcoming month.

➔ From 1-10, how do you feel about the past month?

_____

➔ What was your favorite thing that happened this past month. Describe it:

_____
_____
_____
_____

➔ What are the three biggest lessons you learned from the past month?

_____
_____
_____
_____

➔ Review the past month of your PlanBook and assess your priorities. Did you accomplish what you set out to? Are you happy with your results and how you spent your time? If not, what steps can you take to improve in the upcoming month?

_____
_____
_____
_____
_____

→ What is one thing you accomplished this past month? What did you do to celebrate your accomplishment?

_____
_____
_____
_____
_____
_____

→ Do you feel that you are still in alignment with your goals? If not, explain why and what's changed for you in the past month.

_____
_____
_____
_____
_____
_____

→ Name three things you can improve on this upcoming month to keep you moving towards your goals. List concrete action steps you can take towards making these improvements.

_____
_____
_____
_____
_____
_____

→ Who or what are you especially grateful for from this past month? Describe in detail your gratitude and how it makes you feel. If it's a person, what is a way you can express your gratitude to them?

_____
_____
_____
_____
_____
_____

Notes

Thoughts | Ideas | Brainstorming | Brilliance

Notes

Thoughts | Ideas | Brainstorming | Brilliance

February's Idea Bucket

THEME: _____
(copied from sandbox)

→ ~~Brainstorm~~ all the different things you could talk/write/blog/video about this month's theme. Get specific. The more specific, the better.

Put your ideas in the bucket. Refer back to often for inspiration.

WEEKLY PLAN....

Lets talk FREE STUFF, shall we ...

①

②

③

④

MESMERIZING GOES HERE MATERIAL

...Everyone loves free stuff. It's what attracts people to your business. In each box above, choose a topic of the week that revolves around your theme of the month. HINT: Check your idea bucket.

→ Write down what you will do to share that content with others.

TIP: Free content are things like blog posts, infographics, lists, opt-ins, podcasts, videos, webinars, etc.

→ Make the commitment and add them to your planner with due dates.

this month's February 2017

theme	sunday	monday	tuesday
reminders	5	6	7
	12	13	14
goals	19	20	21
$	26	27	28

things to get done this month

this month's newsletter(s)

mailing date(s):

topic:

related free content:

ways to generate buzz:

wednesday	thursday	friday	saturday
1	2	3	4
8	9	10	11
15	16	17	18
22	23	24	25

ideas | brainstorming | brilliance

January 2017

this week's focus

30 monday

good stuff

31 tuesday

1 wednesday

"Don't get caught up with flashy tools. Use what you have, ship it, make money, then get the nice tools."

Lynette Chandler
TechBasedMarketing.com

email/newsletter/promo ideas

February 2017

2 thursday	to-do's
	3 most important tasks
	1.
	2.
	3.

3 friday

4 saturday **5 sunday**

ideas | brainstorming | brilliance

February 2017

this week's focus	⑥ monday

good stuff | ⑦ tuesday

"The journey to joyful living is not a one time destination, but a daily pursuit of the Joy Giver Himself."

Terry Gassett
HereToThereLifeCoaching.com

⑧ wednesday

email/newsletter/promo ideas

9 thursday

to-do's

3 most important tasks

- [ ] 1.
- [ ] 2.
- [ ] 3.
- [ ]
- [ ]
- [ ]
- [ ]
- [ ]
- [ ]
- [ ]
- [ ]
- [ ]
- [ ]
- [ ]
- [ ]
- [ ]
- [ ]

10 friday

11 saturday   **12** sunday

ideas | brainstorming | brilliance

February 2017

this week's focus	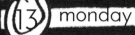 13 monday

good stuff	14 tuesday

"Get curious and dig into the resistance you feel. Underneath you'll find gold." Gina Fresquez Gina-Louise.com	15 wednesday

email/newsletter/promo ideas

16 thursday

to-do's

3 most important tasks

1.
2.
3.

17 friday

18 saturday

19 sunday

ideas | brainstorming | brilliance

February 2017

this week's focus	20 monday
✬	
good stuff	21 tuesday
♡	
"Marketing is what you do. Branding is what you are!" Lou Bortone LouBortone.com	22 wednesday

email/newsletter/promo ideas

23 thursday

to-do's

3 most important tasks

1.
2.
3.

24 friday

25 saturday

26 sunday

ideas | brainstorming | brilliance

Monthly Checkin !

This is powerful stuff! ➡️

"It is only in the review of your performance that you can have breakthroughs." -Steven Griffith

IMPORTANT: At the end of every month, take the time to reflect on how you felt about the past month, what you accomplished and what you feel you could improve on in the upcoming month.

➡️ From 1-10, how do you feel about the past month?

_____

➡️ What was your favorite thing that happened this past month. Describe it:

_____
_____
_____
_____

➡️ What are the three biggest lessons you learned from the past month?

_____
_____
_____
_____

➡️ Review the past month of your PlanBook and assess your priorities. Did you accomplish what you set out to? Are you happy with your results and how you spent your time? If not, what steps can you take to improve in the upcoming month?

_____
_____
_____
_____
_____
_____

→ What is one thing you accomplished this past month? What did you do to celebrate your accomplishment?

_____

_____

_____

_____

_____

_____

→ Do you feel that you are still in alignment with your goals? If not, explain why and what's changed for you in the past month.

_____

_____

_____

_____

_____

_____

→ Name three things you can improve on this upcoming month to keep you moving towards your goals. List concrete action steps you can take towards making these improvements.

_____

_____

_____

_____

_____

_____

→ Who or what are you especially grateful for from this past month? Describe in detail your gratitude and how it makes you feel. If it's a person, what is a way you can express your gratitude to them?

_____

_____

_____

_____

_____

_____

Notes

Thoughts | Ideas | Brainstorming | Brilliance

Notes

Thoughts | Ideas | Brainstorming | Brilliance

March's Idea Bucket

THEME: _____
(copied from sandbox)

→ Brainstorm all the different things you could talk/write/blog/video about this month's theme. Get specific. The more specific, the better.

Put your ideas in the bucket. Refer back to often for inspiration.

WEEKLY PLAN.....

Let's talk FREE stuff, shall we ...

①

②

MESMERIZING
GOES HERE
MATERIAL

④

③

...Everyone loves free stuff. It's what attracts people to your business. In each box above, choose a topic of the week that revolves around your theme of the month. HINT: Check your idea bucket.

→Write down what you will do to share that content with others.

TIP: Free content are things like blog posts, infographics, lists, opt-ins, podcasts, videos, webinars, etc.

→Make the commitment and add them to your planner with due dates.

this month's **March** 2017

theme	sunday	monday	tuesday
reminders	5	6	7
	12	13	14
goals	19	20	21
$	26	27	28

things to get done this month

this month's newsletter(s)

mailing date(s):

topic:

related free content:

ways to generate buzz:

wednesday	thursday	friday	saturday
1	2	3	4
8	9	10	11
15	16	17	18
22	23	24	25
29	30	31	

ideas | brainstorming | brilliance

March 2017

this week's focus	27 monday

good stuff	28 tuesday

"You only have to do the first time once." Lin Gorenkoff TheSelectivelySilentChild.com	1 wednesday

email/newsletter/promo ideas

March 2017

2 thursday	to-do's
	3 most important tasks
	1.
	2.
	3.

3 friday

4 saturday　　**5 sunday**

ideas | brainstorming | brilliance

March 2017

this week's focus

6 monday

good stuff

7 tuesday

8 wednesday

"The highest level of
success comes from
conviction, commitment
and persistence."

Debra Jason
MillionaireMarketingonaShoestringBudget.com

email/newsletter/promo ideas

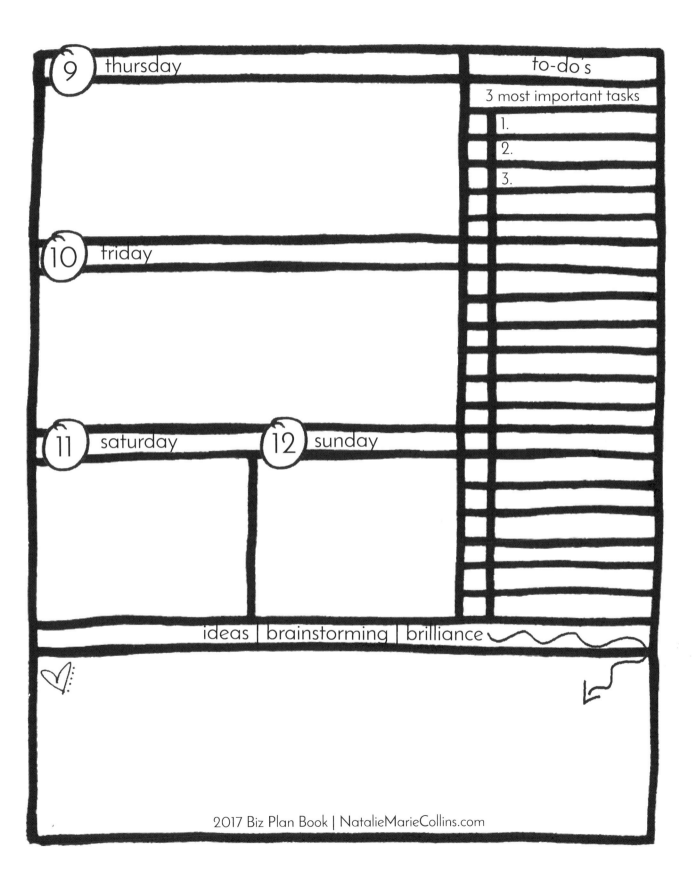

9 thursday

to-do's

3 most important tasks

1.

2.

3.

10 friday

11 saturday   12 sunday

ideas | brainstorming | brilliance

March 2017

this week's focus	13 monday
good stuff	14 tuesday
"Your body has its own wisdom—listen to its messages. Unlike the mind, it speaks non-linguistically & won't argue with itself." Kay Rice KayRice.com	15 wednesday

email/newsletter/promo ideas

16 thursday

17 friday

18 saturday

19 sunday

to-do's

3 most important tasks

1.
2.
3.

ideas | brainstorming | brilliance

March 2017

this week's focus	20 monday

good stuff	21 tuesday

"The Law of Attraction Only Works with Action!" Juliet Easton JulietEaston.com	22 wednesday

email/newsletter/promo ideas

23 thursday	to-do's
	3 most important tasks
	1.
	2.
	3.

24 friday

25 saturday | **26 sunday**

ideas | brainstorming | brilliance

March 2017

this week's focus

27 monday

good stuff

28 tuesday

29 wednesday

"Never take yourself too seriously, but be serious about your passion and livelihood."

Paul Klein
TitanWebMarketing.com

email/newsletter/promo ideas

30	thursday	to-do's

3 most important tasks

1.
2.
3.

31	friday

1	saturday	2	sunday

ideas | brainstorming | brilliance

Monthly Checkin !

This is powerful stuff! →

"It is only in the review of your performance that you can have breakthroughs." -Steven Griffith

IMPORTANT: At the end of every month, take the time to reflect on how you felt about the past month, what you accomplished and what you feel you could improve on in the upcoming month.

→ From 1-10, how do you feel about the past month?

_____

→ What was your favorite thing that happened this past month. Describe it:

_____
_____
_____
_____

→ What are the three biggest lessons you learned from the past month?

_____
_____
_____
_____

→ Review the past month of your PlanBook and assess your priorities. Did you accomplish what you set out to? Are you happy with your results and how you spent your time? If not, what steps can you take to improve in the upcoming month?

_____
_____
_____
_____
_____
_____

→ What is one thing you accomplished this past month? What did you do to celebrate your accomplishment?

_____
_____
_____
_____
_____

→ Do you feel that you are still in alignment with your goals? If not, explain why and what's changed for you in the past month.

_____
_____
_____
_____
_____

→ Name three things you can improve on this upcoming month to keep you moving towards your goals. List concrete action steps you can take towards making these improvements.

_____
_____
_____
_____
_____

→ Who or what are you especially grateful for from this past month? Describe in detail your gratitude and how it makes you feel. If it's a person, what is a way you can express your gratitude to them?

_____
_____
_____
_____
_____

Notes

Thoughts | Ideas | Brainstorming | Brilliance

Notes

Thoughts | Ideas | Brainstorming | Brilliance

2nd Quarter

The Passion Subject is: _____

→ Brainstorm all the different things you could share with others about this subject and add them to your idea bucket below.

... IDEAS ARE SAFE HERE ...

NEXT:

◉ Circle 3 things that meet these criteria :

→ Would make a great report, ebook, mini-course or some other kind of smaller product or service. ($97 or less)

→ People want to learn about it or receive it.

→ Is something you could create in 1-2 weeks.

2nd Quarter's Focus: _____
(passion subject goes here)

→ In each box below, add 1 mini-product idea from the previous page. This is the product you will create for that month (before that month begins is best). This is also your theme for that month.
More on themes coming up.

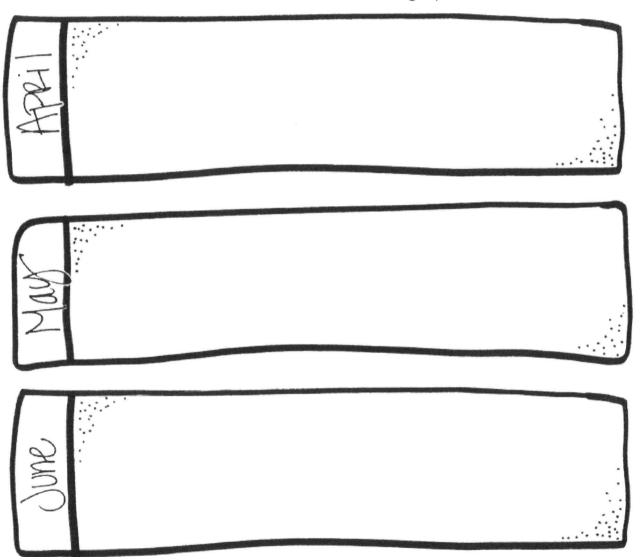

April

May

June

Each box is your sandbox of ideas to play in for that month.

NOTE: Creating your product the month before will increase your success.

Turn the page for more fun ...

April's Idea Bucket

THEME: _____
(copied from sandbox)

→ **Brainstorm** all the different things you could talk/write/blog/video about this month's theme. Get specific. The more specific, the better.

Put your ideas in the bucket. Refer back to often for inspiration.

WEEKLY PLAN...

Lets talk FREE stuff, shall we ...

①

②

MESMERIZING GOES HERE MATERIAL

④

③

...Everyone loves free stuff. It's what attracts people to your business. In each box above, choose a topic of the week that revolves around your theme of the month. HINT: Check your idea bucket.

→Write down what you will do to share that content with others.

TIP: Free content are things like blog posts, infographics, lists, opt-ins, podcasts, videos, webinars, etc.

→Make the commitment and add them to your planner with due dates.

this month's **APRIL** 2017

theme	sunday	monday	tuesday
reminders	2	3	4
	9	10	11
goals	16	17	18
$	23 / 30	24	25

things to get done this month

this month's newsletter(s)

mailing date(s):

topic:

related free content:

ways to generate buzz:

wednesday	thursday	friday	saturday
			1
5	6	7	8
12	13	14	15
19	20	21	22
26	27	28	29

ideas | brainstorming | brilliance

APRIL 2017

this week's focus	**3** monday
good stuff	**4** tuesday
"Tomorrow is coming regardless how long it takes. Your job is to be around to greet it when it does." Khrys Vaughan TheRedUmbrellaSociety.com	**5** wednesday

email/newsletter/promo ideas

6	thursday	to-do's

3 most important tasks

1.
2.
3.

7	friday

8	saturday	9	sunday

ideas | brainstorming | brilliance

April 2017

this week's focus	 10 monday
good stuff	11 tuesday

12 wednesday

"I envision a world
in which all people
are valued for their
unique contribution."

Rhonda Knight Boyle
RhondaBoyle.com

email/newsletter/promo ideas

13 thursday

to-do's

3 most important tasks

1.

2.

3.

14 friday

15 saturday   **16** sunday

ideas | brainstorming | brilliance

APRIL 2017

this week's focus	 17 monday
good stuff	 18 tuesday
"BLOOM" where you're planted..." Marilyn Morange getoiling.com/marilynmorange	19 wednesday

email/newsletter/promo ideas

20 thursday

to-do's

3 most important tasks

1.
2.
3.

21 friday

22 saturday

23 sunday

ideas | brainstorming | brilliance

April 2017

this week's focus	24 monday
good stuff	25 tuesday
	26 wednesday
"It takes a lot of guts to go out there and radiate your essence." Natalie Marie Collins NatalieMarieCollins.com	

email/newsletter/promo ideas

27 thursday

to-do's

3 most important tasks

1.

2.

3.

28 friday

29 saturday

30 sunday

ideas | brainstorming | brilliance

Monthly Checkin !

This is powerful stuff! ⟶

"It is only in the review of your performance that you can have breakthroughs." -Steven Griffith

IMPORTANT: At the end of every month, take the time to reflect on how you felt about the past month, what you accomplished and what you feel you could improve on in the upcoming month.

⟶ From 1-10, how do you feel about the past month?

_____

⟶ What was your favorite thing that happened this past month. Describe it:

_____
_____
_____
_____
_____

⟶ What are the three biggest lessons you learned from the past month?

_____
_____
_____
_____

⟶ Review the past month of your PlanBook and assess your priorities. Did you accomplish what you set out to? Are you happy with your results and how you spent your time? If not, what steps can you take to improve in the upcoming month?

_____
_____
_____
_____
_____
_____

→ What is one thing you accomplished this past month? What did you do to celebrate your accomplishment?

_____

_____

_____

_____

_____

_____

→ Do you feel that you are still in alignment with your goals? If not, explain why and what's changed for you in the past month.

_____

_____

_____

_____

_____

_____

→ Name three things you can improve on this upcoming month to keep you moving towards your goals. List concrete action steps you can take towards making these improvements.

_____

_____

_____

_____

_____

→ Who or what are you especially grateful for from this past month? Describe in detail your gratitude and how it makes you feel. If it's a person, what is a way you can express your gratitude to them?

_____

_____

_____

_____

_____

_____

Notes

Thoughts | Ideas | Brainstorming | Brilliance

Notes

Thoughts | Ideas | Brainstorming | Brilliance

May's Idea Bucket

THEME: _____
(copied from sandbox)

→ **Brainstorm** all the different things you could talk/write/blog/video about this month's theme. Get specific. The more specific, the better.

Put your ideas in the bucket. Refer back to often for inspiration.

WEEKLY PLAN...

Lets talk FREE stuff, shall we ...

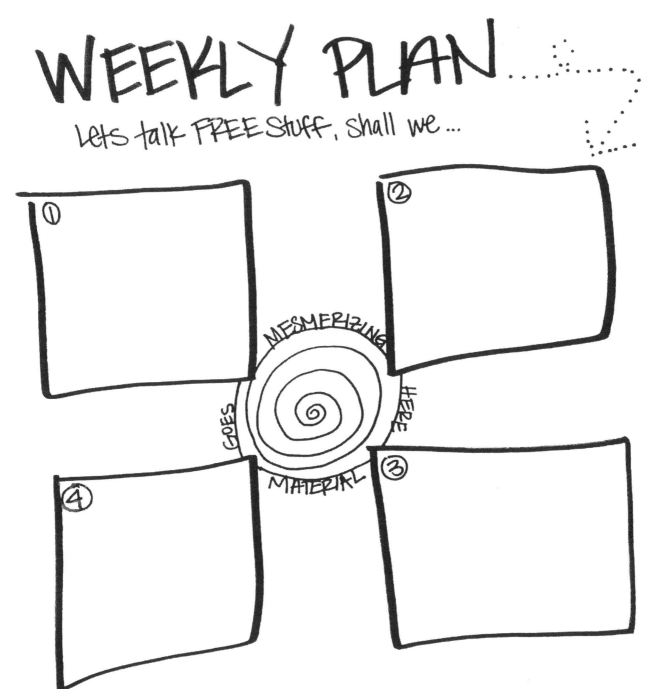

①

②

MESMERIZING
GOES
HERE
MATERIAL

④

③

...Everyone loves free stuff. It's what attracts people to your business. In each box above, choose a topic of the week that revolves around your theme of the month. HINT: Check your idea bucket.

→Write down what you will do to share that content with others.

TIP: Free content are things like blog posts, infographics, lists, opt-ins, podcasts, videos, webinars, etc.

→Make the commitment and add them to your planner with due dates.

this month's *May* 2017

sunday	monday	tuesday
	1	2
7	8	9
14	15	16
21	22	23
28	29	30

theme

reminders

goals

$

things to get done this month

this month's newsletter(s)

mailing date(s):

topic:

related free content:

ways to generate buzz:

wednesday	thursday	friday	saturday
3	4	5	6
10	11	12	13
17	18	19	20
24	25	26	27
31			

ideas | brainstorming | brilliance

May 2017

this week's focus	1 monday

good stuff	2 tuesday

	3 wednesday
"You're too beautiful to be ugly." Eric Thomas ThePurposeMap.com	

email/newsletter/promo ideas

4 thursday	to-do's
	3 most important tasks
	1.
	2.
	3.

5 friday

6 saturday   **7 sunday**

ideas | brainstorming | brilliance

May 2017

this week's focus	8 monday

good stuff	9 tuesday

	10 wednesday
"It's never to late to pursue your dreams, live YOUR life!" Elizabeth Aristeguieta SailAwayGirl.com	

email/newsletter/promo ideas

11 thursday

to-do's

3 most important tasks

1.
2.
3.

12 friday

13 saturday

14 sunday

ideas | brainstorming | brilliance

May 2017

| this week's focus | 15 monday |
| good stuff | 16 tuesday |

| "Boldly building a business around who you are is about honoring all of you."

Stephanie Calahan
StephanieCalahan.com | 17 wednesday |

email/newsletter/promo ideas

18 thursday

to-do's

3 most important tasks

1.

2.

3.

19 friday

20 saturday

21 sunday

ideas | brainstorming | brilliance

May 2017

this week's focus		22 monday
good stuff		23 tuesday

24 wednesday

"Recovering from the wrong decision builds more character than always making the right one."

Karen Banes
KarenBanes.com

email/newsletter/promo ideas

25 thursday

to-do's

3 most important tasks

1.

2.

3.

26 friday

27 saturday   **28** sunday

ideas | brainstorming | brilliance

Monthly Checkin !

This is powerful stuff! ➔

"It is only in the review of your performance that you can have breakthroughs." -Steven Griffith

IMPORTANT: At the end of every month, take the time to reflect on how you felt about the past month, what you accomplished and what you feel you could improve on in the upcoming month.

➔ From 1-10, how do you feel about the past month?

_____

➔ What was your favorite thing that happened this past month. Describe it:

_____
_____
_____
_____

➔ What are the three biggest lessons you learned from the past month?

_____
_____
_____
_____

➔ Review the past month of your PlanBook and assess your priorities. Did you accomplish what you set out to? Are you happy with your results and how you spent your time? If not, what steps can you take to improve in the upcoming month?

_____
_____
_____
_____
_____
_____

→ What is one thing you accomplished this past month? What did you do to celebrate your accomplishment?

_____

_____

_____

_____

_____

→ Do you feel that you are still in alignment with your goals? If not, explain why and what's changed for you in the past month.

_____

_____

_____

_____

_____

→ Name three things you can improve on this upcoming month to keep you moving towards your goals. List concrete action steps you can take towards making these improvements.

_____

_____

_____

_____

_____

→ Who or what are you especially grateful for from this past month? Describe in detail your gratitude and how it makes you feel. If it's a person, what is a way you can express your gratitude to them?

_____

_____

_____

_____

_____

Notes

Thoughts | Ideas | Brainstorming | Brilliance

Notes

Thoughts | Ideas | Brainstorming | Brilliance

June's Idea Bucket

THEME: _____
(copied from sandbox)

→ Brainstorm all the different things you could talk/write/blog/video about this month's theme. Get specific. The more specific, the better.

Put your ideas in the bucket. Refer back to often for inspiration.

WEEKLY PLAN...

Lets talk FREE stuff, shall we ...

①

②

MESMERIZING GOES HERE MATERIAL

③

④

...Everyone loves free stuff. It's what attracts people to your business. In each box above, choose a topic of the week that revolves around your theme of the month. HINT: Check your idea bucket.

→ Write down what you will do to share that content with others.

TIP: Free content are things like blog posts, infographics, lists, opt-ins, podcasts, videos, webinars, etc.

→ Make the commitment and add them to your planner with due dates.

this month's  June 2017

theme

reminders

goals

$

sunday	monday	tuesday
4	5	6
11	12	13
18	19	20
25	26	27

things to get done this month

this month's newsletter(s)

mailing date(s):

topic:

related free content:

ways to generate buzz:

wednesday	thursday	friday	saturday
	1	2	3
7	8	9	10
14	15	16	17
21	22	23	24
28	29	30	

ideas | brainstorming | brilliance

June 2017

| this week's focus | | 29 monday |

| good stuff | | 30 tuesday |

| "Until you take ACTION, everything you invest in is worthless.."

Kristen Joy
TheBookNinja.com | | 31 wednesday |

email/newsletter/promo ideas

1 thursday

to-do's

3 most important tasks

1.

2.

3.

2 friday

3 saturday   **4** sunday

ideas | brainstorming | brilliance

June 2017

this week's focus

good stuff

"Unknown happiness can be perceived as a threat to familiar misery."

Tony Laidig
TonyLaidig.com

 5 monday

 6 tuesday

  7 wednesday

email/newsletter/promo ideas

8 thursday

to-do's

3 most important tasks

1.
2.
3.

9 friday

10 saturday   **11** sunday

ideas | brainstorming | brilliance

June 2017

this week's focus	12 monday

good stuff	13 tuesday

"Do for a year what others won't; Live the way others can't, forever." Connie Ragen Green ConnieRagenGreen.com	14 wednesday

email/newsletter/promo ideas

15 thursday

to-do's

3 most important tasks

1.
2.
3.

16 friday

17 saturday

18 sunday

ideas | brainstorming | brilliance

June 2017

this week's focus	19 monday
good stuff	20 tuesday
"I was recently asked, 'What do you do as a coach?' I replied, 'I love people to success!'" D'vorah Lansky ReachMoreReaders.com	21 wednesday

email/newsletter/promo ideas

22 thursday

to-do's

3 most important tasks

1.
2.
3.

23 friday

24 saturday

25 sunday

ideas | brainstorming | brilliance

June 2017

| this week's focus | | 26 monday |
| good stuff | | 27 tuesday |

28 wednesday

"There's rarely an easy way out. The easy way is usually in, so open up, and let yourself be vulnerable."

Mariya Karchevskaya
TheGoodDesigner.net

email/newsletter/promo ideas

29 thursday

to-do's

3 most important tasks

1.
2.
3.

30 friday

1 saturday

2 sunday

ideas | brainstorming | brilliance

Monthly Checkin !

This is powerful stuff! ➡

"It is only in the review of your performance that you can have breakthroughs." -Steven Griffith

IMPORTANT: At the end of every month, take the time to reflect on how you felt about the past month, what you accomplished and what you feel you could improve on in the upcoming month.

➡ From 1-10, how do you feel about the past month?

_____

➡ What was your favorite thing that happened this past month. Describe it:

_____
_____
_____
_____
_____

➡ What are the three biggest lessons you learned from the past month?

_____
_____
_____
_____

➡ Review the past month of your PlanBook and assess your priorities. Did you accomplish what you set out to? Are you happy with your results and how you spent your time? If not, what steps can you take to improve in the upcoming month?

_____
_____
_____
_____
_____

→ What is one thing you accomplished this past month? What did you do to celebrate your accomplishment?

_____

_____

_____

_____

_____

→ Do you feel that you are still in alignment with your goals? If not, explain why and what's changed for you in the past month.

_____

_____

_____

_____

_____

→ Name three things you can improve on this upcoming month to keep you moving towards your goals. List concrete action steps you can take towards making these improvements.

_____

_____

_____

_____

_____

→ Who or what are you especially grateful for from this past month? Describe in detail your gratitude and how it makes you feel. If it's a person, what is a way you can express your gratitude to them?

_____

_____

_____

_____

_____

_____

Notes

Thoughts | Ideas | Brainstorming | Brilliance

Notes

Thoughts | Ideas | Brainstorming | Brilliance

3rd Quarter

The Passion Subject is: _____

→ Brainstorm all the different things you could share with others about this subject and add them to your idea bucket below.

... IDEAS ARE SAFE HERE ...

NEXT:

◉ Circle 3 things that meet these criteria :

→ Would make a great report, ebook, mini-course or some other kind of smaller product or service. ($97 or less)

→ People want to learn about it or receive it.

→ Is something you could create in 1-2 weeks.

3rd Quarter's Focus: _____
(passion subject goes here)

→ In each box below, add 1 mini-product idea from the previous page. This is the product you will create for that month (before that month begins is best). This is also your theme for that month.
More on themes coming up.

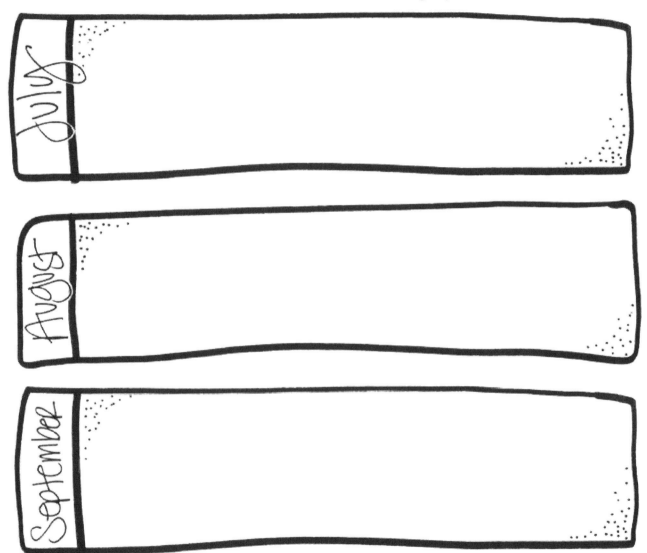

July

August

September

Each box is your sandbox of ideas to play in for that month.

NOTE: Creating your product the month before will increase your success.

Turn the page for more fun ...

July's Idea Bucket

THEME: _____
(copied from sandbox)

→ **Brainstorm** all the different things you could talk/write/blog/video about this month's theme. Get specific. The more specific, the better.

Put your ideas in the bucket. Refer back to often for inspiration.

WEEKLY PLAN...

Lets talk FREE stuff, shall we...

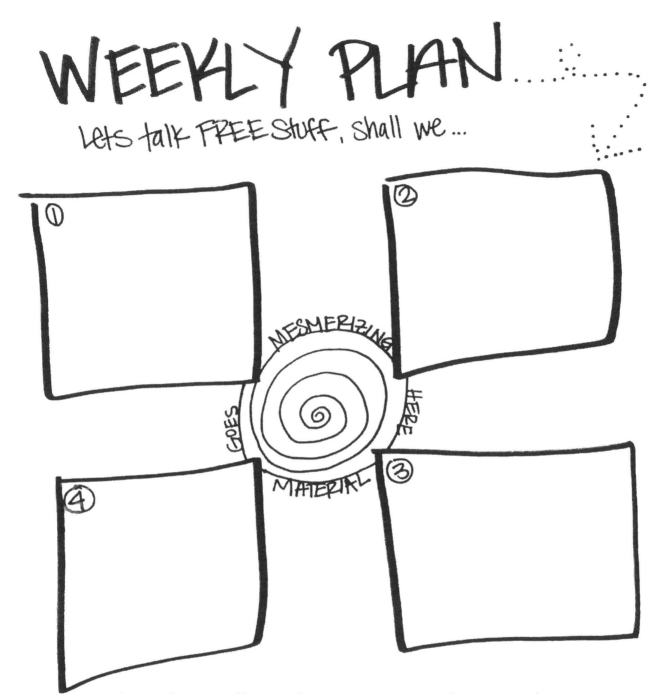

...Everyone loves free stuff. It's what attracts people to your business. In each box above, choose a topic of the week that revolves around your theme of the month. HINT: Check your idea bucket.

→Write down what you will do to share that content with others.

TIP: Free content are things like blog posts, infographics, lists, opt-ins, podcasts, videos, webinars, etc.

→Make the commitment and add them to your planner with due dates.

this month's July 2017

theme

reminders

goals

$

sunday	monday	tuesday
2	3	4
9	10	11
16	17	18
23 / 30	24 / 31	25

things to get done this month

this month's newsletter(s)

mailing date(s):

topic:

related free content:

ways to generate buzz:

wednesday	thursday	friday	saturday
			1
5	6	7	8
12	13	14	15
19	20	21	22
26	27	28	29

ideas | brainstorming | brilliance

July  2017

this week's focus	3 monday
good stuff	4 tuesday
"The harder I work, the luckier I get!" Liz Fulcher AromaticWisdomInstitute.com	5 wednesday

email/newsletter/promo ideas

6 thursday

to-do's

3 most important tasks

1.

2.

3.

7 friday

8 saturday **9** sunday

ideas | brainstorming | brilliance

July 2017

this week's focus	⑩ monday
good stuff	⑪ tuesday
"If chocolate doesn't solve it, action will!" Kristen Joy TheBookNinja.com	⑫ wednesday

email/newsletter/promo ideas

13 thursday

14 friday

15 saturday

16 sunday

to-do's

3 most important tasks

□ 1.
□ 2.
□ 3.
□
□
□
□
□
□
□
□
□
□
□
□
□
□

ideas | brainstorming | brilliance

July 2017

this week's focus **17** monday

good stuff **18** tuesday

"Say YES to more things - more often - that set your soul on fire."

Randi Pierce
RandiPierce.com

19 wednesday

email/newsletter/promo ideas

20	thursday	to-do's

3 most important tasks

1.
2.
3.

21 friday

22 saturday   **23** sunday

ideas | brainstorming | brilliance

July 2017

this week's focus	**24** monday
good stuff	**25** tuesday
	26 wednesday

"All you really need is laughter and prayer."

Leslie Bouldin
ljbouldin.com

email/newsletter/promo ideas

27 thursday		to-do's
		3 most important tasks
		1.
		2.
		3.

28 friday

29 saturday	30 sunday

ideas | brainstorming | brilliance

Monthly Checkin !

This is powerful stuff! →

"It is only in the review of your performance that you can have breakthroughs." -Steven Griffith

IMPORTANT: At the end of every month, take the time to reflect on how you felt about the past month, what you accomplished and what you feel you could improve on in the upcoming month.

→ From 1-10, how do you feel about the past month?

_____

→ What was your favorite thing that happened this past month. Describe it:

_____
_____
_____
_____
_____

→ What are the three biggest lessons you learned from the past month?

_____
_____
_____
_____

→ Review the past month of your PlanBook and assess your priorities. Did you accomplish what you set out to? Are you happy with your results and how you spent your time? If not, what steps can you take to improve in the upcoming month?

_____
_____
_____
_____
_____
_____

→ What is one thing you accomplished this past month? What did you do to celebrate your accomplishment?

_____

_____

_____

_____

_____

→ Do you feel that you are still in alignment with your goals? If not, explain why and what's changed for you in the past month.

_____

_____

_____

_____

_____

→ Name three things you can improve on this upcoming month to keep you moving towards your goals. List concrete action steps you can take towards making these improvements.

_____

_____

_____

_____

→ Who or what are you especially grateful for from this past month? Describe in detail your gratitude and how it makes you feel. If it's a person, what is a way you can express your gratitude to them?

_____

_____

_____

_____

_____

Notes

Thoughts | Ideas | Brainstorming | Brilliance

Notes

Thoughts | Ideas | Brainstorming | Brilliance

August's Idea Bucket

THEME: _____
(copied from sandbox)

→ ~~Brainstorm~~ all the different things you could talk/write/blog/video about this month's theme. Get specific. The more specific, the better.

Put your ideas in the bucket. Refer back to often for inspiration.

WEEKLY PLAN......

Lets talk FREE stuff, shall we ...

①

②

MESMERIZING
GOES
HERE
MATERIAL

④

③

...Everyone loves free stuff. It's what attracts people to your business. In each box above, choose a topic of the week that revolves around your theme of the month. HINT: Check your idea bucket.

→Write down what you will do to share that content with others.

TIP: Free content are things like blog posts, infographics, lists, opt-ins, podcasts, videos, webinars, etc.

→Make the commitment and add them to your planner with due dates.

this month's August 2017

theme

reminders

goals

$

sunday	monday	tuesday
		1
6	7	8
13	14	15
20	21	22
27	28	29

things to get done this month

this month's newsletter(s)

mailing date(s):

topic:

related free content:

ways to generate buzz:

wednesday	thursday	friday	saturday
2	3	4	5
9	10	11	12
16	17	18	19
23	24	25	26
30	31		

ideas | brainstorming | brilliance

August 2017

this week's focus	31 monday
☆	

good stuff	1 tuesday
♡	

"Done is better than perfect!" Robin Smith BeSocialGetSuccess.com	2 wednesday

email/newsletter/promo ideas

3 thursday

to-do's

3 most important tasks

1.
2.
3.

4 friday

5 saturday

6 sunday

ideas | brainstorming | brilliance

August 2017

this week's focus	7 monday

good stuff	8 tuesday

"Unless you have a core focus based on something you truly believe in, you have a hobby, not a business." Lee Collins Lee-Collins.com	9 wednesday

email/newsletter/promo ideas

10 thursday

to-do's

3 most important tasks

1.

2.

3.

11 friday

12 saturday

13 sunday

ideas | brainstorming | brilliance

August 2017

this week's focus	14 monday
good stuff	15 tuesday
	16 wednesday

"Even the comfiest comfort zone becomes confining eventually... keep moving!"

Elise Adams
CustomerLoveConsulting.com

email/newsletter/promo ideas

17 thursday	**to-do's**
	3 most important tasks
	1.
	2.
	3.
18 friday	
19 saturday **20** sunday	

ideas | brainstorming | brilliance

August 2017

this week's focus	(21) monday
☆	

good stuff	(22) tuesday

| "Be humble enough to offer support and courageous enough to ask for help."

Jan Riley
YouCreateYou.com	(23) wednesday

email/newsletter/promo ideas

24 thursday

to-do's

3 most important tasks

1.

2.

3.

25 friday

26 saturday

27 sunday

ideas | brainstorming | brilliance

August 2017

this week's focus	28 monday

good stuff	29 tuesday

30 wednesday

"Make people your passion and money will find you."

Brian Basilico
b2b-im.com

email/newsletter/promo ideas

31 thursday		**to-do's**
		3 most important tasks
		☐ 1.
		☐ 2.
		☐ 3.

1 friday

2 saturday

3 sunday

ideas | brainstorming | brilliance

Monthly Checkin !

This is powerful stuff! ➔

"It is only in the review of your performance that you can have breakthroughs." -Steven Griffith

IMPORTANT: At the end of every month, take the time to reflect on how you felt about the past month, what you accomplished and what you feel you could improve on in the upcoming month.

➔ From 1-10, how do you feel about the past month?

_____

➔ What was your favorite thing that happened this past month. Describe it:

_____
_____
_____
_____
_____

➔ What are the three biggest lessons you learned from the past month?

_____
_____
_____
_____

➔ Review the past month of your PlanBook and assess your priorities. Did you accomplish what you set out to? Are you happy with your results and how you spent your time? If not, what steps can you take to improve in the upcoming month?

_____
_____
_____
_____
_____

→ What is one thing you accomplished this past month? What did you do to celebrate your accomplishment?

_____
_____
_____
_____
_____

→ Do you feel that you are still in alignment with your goals? If not, explain why and what's changed for you in the past month.

_____
_____
_____
_____
_____

→ Name three things you can improve on this upcoming month to keep you moving towards your goals. List concrete action steps you can take towards making these improvements.

_____
_____
_____
_____

→ Who or what are you especially grateful for from this past month? Describe in detail your gratitude and how it makes you feel. If it's a person, what is a way you can express your gratitude to them?

_____
_____
_____
_____

Notes

Thoughts | Ideas | Brainstorming | Brilliance

Thoughts | Ideas | Brainstorming | Brilliance

_____

_____

_____

_____

_____

_____

_____

_____

_____

_____

_____

_____

_____

_____

_____

_____

_____

_____

_____

_____

_____

September's Idea Bucket

THEME: _____
(copied from sandbox)

→ **Brainstorm** all the different things you could talk/write/blog/video about this month's theme. Get specific. The more specific, the better.

Put your ideas in the bucket. Refer back to often for inspiration.

WEEKLY PLAN...

Lets talk FREE stuff, shall we...

①   ②

MESMERIZING GOES HERE MATERIAL

④   ③

...Everyone loves free stuff. It's what attracts people to your business. In each box above, choose a topic of the week that revolves around your theme of the month. HINT: Check your idea bucket.

→ Write down what you will do to share that content with others.

     TIP: Free content are things like blog posts, infographics, lists, opt-ins, podcasts, videos, webinars, etc.

→ Make the commitment and add them to your planner with due dates.

this month's **September** 2017

theme	sunday	monday	tuesday
reminders	3	4	5
	10	11	12
goals	17	18	19
$	24	25	26

things to get done this month	this month's newsletter(s)
	mailing date(s):
	topic:
	related free content:
	ways to generate buzz:

wednesday	thursday	friday	saturday
		1	2
6	7	8	9
13	14	15	16
20	21	22	23
27	28	29	30

ideas | brainstorming | brilliance

♥

September 2017

this week's focus	4 monday

good stuff	5 tuesday

| 6 wednesday |

"Find people hungry for what you offer. Don't try to force-feed bacon to a vegan, when there are bacon-lovers EVERYWHERE."

Felicia Slattery
FeliciaSlattery.com

email/newsletter/promo ideas

7 thursday

to-do's

3 most important tasks

1.

2.

3.

8 friday

9 saturday

10 sunday

ideas | brainstorming | brilliance

September 2017

this week's focus	11 monday
good stuff	12 tuesday
"Motivation and change are reversible, but a transformation is permanent. A butterfly will never be a caterpillar again." Nicole Dean NicoleontheNet.com	13 wednesday

email/newsletter/promo ideas

14 thursday

15 friday

16 saturday

17 sunday

to-do's

3 most important tasks

1.
2.
3.

ideas | brainstorming | brilliance

September 2017

this week's focus	18 monday

good stuff	19 tuesday

"Every day there are people searching and praying for the solutions that only you can provide." Stephanie Calahan StephanieCalahan.com	20 wednesday

email/newsletter/promo ideas

21 thursday

to-do's

3 most important tasks

1.
2.
3.

22 friday

23 saturday

24 sunday

ideas | brainstorming | brilliance

September 2017

this week's focus	25 monday

good stuff	26 tuesday

"Love, Joy, Surprise and Delight are your NATURAL state of being!" Therese Sparby ThereseSparby.com	27 wednesday

email/newsletter/promo ideas

28 thursday

29 friday

30 saturday

1 sunday

to-do's

3 most important tasks

1.
2.
3.

ideas | brainstorming | brilliance

Monthly Checkin !

This is powerful stuff! →

"It is only in the review of your performance that you can have breakthroughs." -Steven Griffith

IMPORTANT: At the end of every month, take the time to reflect on how you felt about the past month, what you accomplished and what you feel you could improve on in the upcoming month.

→ From 1-10, how do you feel about the past month?

_____

→ What was your favorite thing that happened this past month. Describe it:

_____
_____
_____
_____

→ What are the three biggest lessons you learned from the past month?

_____
_____
_____
_____

→ Review the past month of your PlanBook and assess your priorities. Did you accomplish what you set out to? Are you happy with your results and how you spent your time? If not, what steps can you take to improve in the upcoming month?

_____
_____
_____
_____
_____

→ What is one thing you accomplished this past month? What did you do to celebrate your accomplishment?

_____

_____

_____

_____

_____

→ Do you feel that you are still in alignment with your goals? If not, explain why and what's changed for you in the past month.

_____

_____

_____

_____

_____

→ Name three things you can improve on this upcoming month to keep you moving towards your goals. List concrete action steps you can take towards making these improvements.

_____

_____

_____

_____

_____

→ Who or what are you especially grateful for from this past month? Describe in detail your gratitude and how it makes you feel. If it's a person, what is a way you can express your gratitude to them?

_____

_____

_____

_____

_____

Notes

Thoughts | Ideas | Brainstorming | Brilliance

Thoughts | Ideas | Brainstorming | Brilliance

4th Quarter

The Passion Subject is: _____

→ Brainstorm all the different things you could share with others about this subject and add them to your idea bucket below.

... IDEAS ARE SAFE HERE ...

NEXT:

◉ Circle 3 things that meet these criteria :

→ Would make a great report, ebook, mini-course or some other kind of smaller product or service. ($97 or less)

→ People want to learn about it or receive it.

→ Is something you could create in 1-2 weeks.

Need Help? →

4th Quarter's Focus: _____

(passion subject goes here)

→ In each box below, add 1 mini-product idea from the previous page. This is the product you will create for that month (before that month begins is best). This is also your theme for that month.
More on themes coming up.

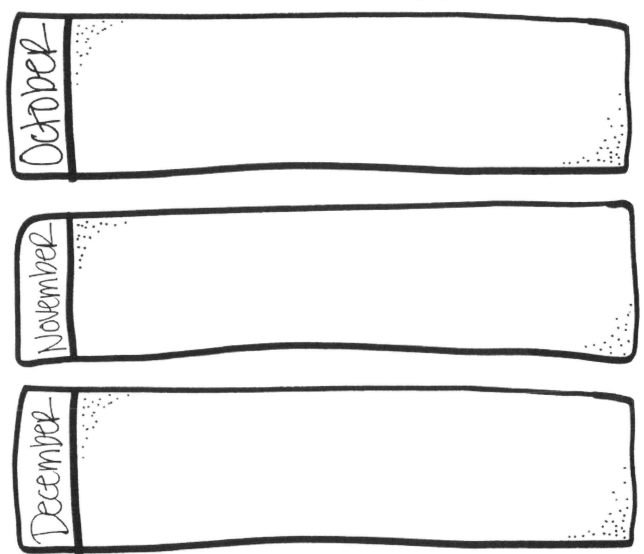

Each box is your sandbox of ideas to play in for that month.

NOTE: Creating your product the month before will increase your success.

Turn the page for more fun ...

Join the free quarterly planning party at: NatalieMarieCollins.com/party

October's Idea Bucket

THEME: _____
(copied from sandbox)

→ **Brainstorm** all the different things you could talk/write/blog/video about this month's theme. Get specific. The more specific, the better.

Put your ideas in the bucket. Refer back to often for inspiration.

WEEKLY PLAN...

Lets talk FREE STUFF, shall we...

①

②

MESMERIZING GOES HERE MATERIAL

③

④

...Everyone loves free stuff. It's what attracts people to your business. In each box above, choose a topic of the week that revolves around your theme of the month. HINT: Check your idea bucket.

→ Write down what you will do to share that content with others.

TIP: Free content are things like blog posts, infographics, lists, opt-ins, podcasts, videos, webinars, etc.

→ Make the commitment and add them to your planner with due dates.

this month's **October** 2017

theme

sunday	monday	tuesday
1	2	3
8	9	10
15	16	17
22	23	24
29	30	31

reminders

goals

$

things to get done this month

this month's newsletter(s)

mailing date(s):

topic:

related free content:

ways to generate buzz:

wednesday	thursday	friday	saturday
4	5	6	7
11	12	13	14
18	19	20	21
25	26	27	228

ideas | brainstorming | brilliance

October 2017

this week's focus	2 monday
good stuff	3 tuesday
"A warm smile is the universal language of kindness." William Arthur Ward	4 wednesday

email/newsletter/promo ideas

5 thursday

6 friday

7 saturday

8 sunday

to-do's

3 most important tasks

1.
2.
3.

ideas | brainstorming | brilliance

October 2017

| this week's focus | 9 monday |

| good stuff | 10 tuesday |

| 11 wednesday |

"Plan to spend time doing the things you love or you will spend your life doing things other people love."

Robin Smith
BeSocialGetSuccess.com

email/newsletter/promo ideas

2017 Biz Plan Book | NatalieMarieCollins.com

12 thursday	to-do's
	3 most important tasks
	1.
	2.
	3.
13 friday	
14 saturday / **15 sunday**	

ideas | brainstorming | brilliance

October 2017

this week's focus	16 monday
good stuff	17 tuesday
"When the Student is ready, the Teacher will appear!" Liz Fulcher AromaticWisdomInstitute.com	18 wednesday

email/newsletter/promo ideas

19 thursday		to-do's
		3 most important tasks
		1.
		2.
		3.

20 friday

21 saturday   **22** sunday

ideas | brainstorming | brilliance

October 2017

this week's focus	23 monday
good stuff	24 tuesday
"Follow your Bliss! If others don't like it, they can't have any." R Steven Thompson FourDirectionsMarketing.com	25 wednesday

email/newsletter/promo ideas

26 thursday

to-do's

3 most important tasks

1.
2.
3.

27 friday

28 saturday   **29** sunday

ideas | brainstorming | brilliance

Monthly Checkin !

This is powerful stuff! ➔

> "It is only in the review of your performance that you can have breakthroughs." -Steven Griffith

IMPORTANT: At the end of every month, take the time to reflect on how you felt about the past month, what you accomplished and what you feel you could improve on in the upcoming month.

➔ From 1-10, how do you feel about the past month?

_____

➔ What was your favorite thing that happened this past month. Describe it:

_____
_____
_____
_____

➔ What are the three biggest lessons you learned from the past month?

_____
_____
_____
_____

➔ Review the past month of your PlanBook and assess your priorities. Did you accomplish what you set out to? Are you happy with your results and how you spent your time? If not, what steps can you take to improve in the upcoming month?

_____
_____
_____
_____
_____
_____

→ What is one thing you accomplished this past month? What did you do to celebrate your accomplishment?

_____

_____

_____

_____

_____

_____

→ Do you feel that you are still in alignment with your goals? If not, explain why and what's changed for you in the past month.

_____

_____

_____

_____

_____

→ Name three things you can improve on this upcoming month to keep you moving towards your goals. List concrete action steps you can take towards making these improvements.

_____

_____

_____

_____

_____

→ Who or what are you especially grateful for from this past month? Describe in detail your gratitude and how it makes you feel. If it's a person, what is a way you can express your gratitude to them?

_____

_____

_____

_____

_____

Notes

Thoughts | Ideas | Brainstorming | Brilliance

Notes

Thoughts | Ideas | Brainstorming | Brilliance

November's Idea Bucket

THEME: _____
(copied from sandbox)

→ Brainstorm all the different things you could talk/write/blog/video about this month's theme. Get specific. The more specific, the better.

Put your ideas in the bucket. Refer back to often for inspiration.

WEEKLY PLAN...

Lets talk FREE STUFF, shall we...

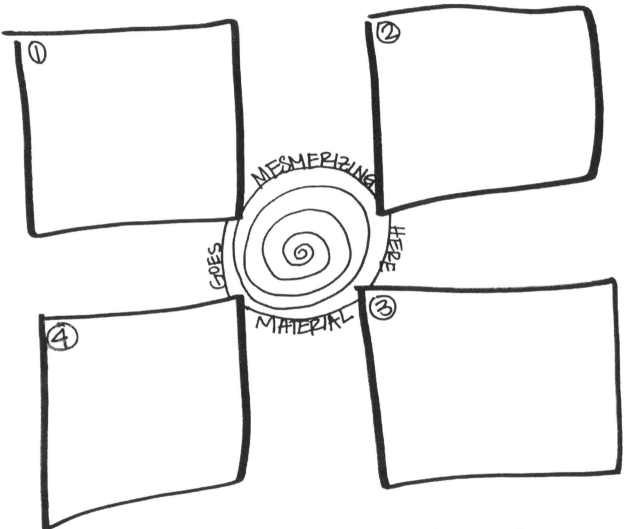

① ② ③ ④

MESMERIZING GOES HERE MATERIAL

...Everyone loves free stuff. It's what attracts people to your business. In each box above, choose a topic of the week that revolves around your theme of the month. HINT: Check your idea bucket.

→ Write down what you will do to share that content with others.

TIP: Free content are things like blog posts, infographics, lists, opt-ins, podcasts, videos, webinars, etc.

→ Make the commitment and add them to your planner with due dates.

this month's November 2017

theme	sunday	monday	tuesday
reminders	5	6	7
	12	13	14
goals	19	20	21
$	26	27	28

things to get done this month

this month's newsletter(s)

mailing date(s):

topic:

related free content:

ways to generate buzz:

wednesday	thursday	friday	saturday
1 Order Biz Plan Book 2018 Edition!	2	3	4
8	9	10	11
15	16	17	18
22	23	24	25
29	30		

ideas | brainstorming | brilliance

♡

November 2017

this week's focus	 **30** monday

good stuff	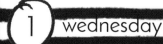 **31** tuesday

| "Your talent is God's gift to you. What you do with it is your gift back to God."

Shelley Hitz
ShelleyHitz.com | **1** wednesday |

email/newsletter/promo ideas

2 thursday

3 friday

4 saturday

5 sunday

to-do's

3 most important tasks

1.

2.

3.

ideas | brainstorming | brilliance

November 2017

this week's focus	6 monday

good stuff	7 tuesday

8 wednesday

"Find success by waking up everyday and pushing the limits unwtil you stumble upon something great."

Deanna McAdams
DeannaMcAdams.com

email/newsletter/promo ideas

9 thursday	to-do's
	3 most important tasks
	1.
	2.
	3.

10 friday

11 saturday   **12 sunday**

ideas | brainstorming | brilliance

November 2017

this week's focus	⑬ monday

good stuff	⑭ tuesday

	⑮ wednesday
"Setbacks create the platform from which you can change the world. Become the solution you needed when life was hard." Faydra Koenig AmericasCrisisCoach.com	

email/newsletter/promo ideas

16 thursday

to-do's
3 most important tasks

☐ 1.
☐ 2.
☐ 3.
☐
☐

17 friday

☐
☐
☐
☐
☐

18 saturday   **19** sunday

☐
☐
☐
☐
☐
☐

ideas | brainstorming | brilliance

November 2017

this week's focus	20 monday
good stuff	21 tuesday
"Any idea, plan, or purpose may be placed in the mind through repetition of thought." Napoleon Hill	22 wednesday

email/newsletter/promo ideas

23 thursday

24 friday

25 saturday

26 sunday

to-do's

3 most important tasks

1.
2.
3.

ideas | brainstorming | brilliance

November 2017

this week's focus	27 monday
good stuff	28 tuesday
"Stay Calm and Embrace Grace!" Joyce Vallejo EverydayLiveWell.com	29 wednesday

email/newsletter/promo ideas

30 thursday

to-do's

3 most important tasks

1.

2.

3.

1 friday

Order Biz Plan Book 2018 Edition!

2 saturday

3 sunday

ideas | brainstorming | brilliance

Monthly Checkin !

This is powerful stuff! ➔

"It is only in the review of your performance that you can have breakthroughs." -Steven Griffith

IMPORTANT: At the end of every month, take the time to reflect on how you felt about the past month, what you accomplished and what you feel you could improve on in the upcoming month.

➔ From 1-10, how do you feel about the past month?

_____

➔ What was your favorite thing that happened this past month. Describe it:

_____
_____
_____
_____

➔ What are the three biggest lessons you learned from the past month?

_____
_____
_____
_____

➔ Review the past month of your PlanBook and assess your priorities. Did you accomplish what you set out to? Are you happy with your results and how you spent your time? If not, what steps can you take to improve in the upcoming month?

_____
_____
_____
_____
_____
_____

→ What is one thing you accomplished this past month? What did you do to celebrate your accomplishment?

_____

_____

_____

_____

_____

_____

→ Do you feel that you are still in alignment with your goals? If not, explain why and what's changed for you in the past month.

_____

_____

_____

_____

_____

→ Name three things you can improve on this upcoming month to keep you moving towards your goals. List concrete action steps you can take towards making these improvements.

_____

_____

_____

_____

_____

→ Who or what are you especially grateful for from this past month? Describe in detail your gratitude and how it makes you feel. If it's a person, what is a way you can express your gratitude to them?

_____

_____

_____

_____

_____

Notes

Thoughts | Ideas | Brainstorming | Brilliance

Notes

Thoughts | Ideas | Brainstorming | Brilliance

December's Idea Bucket

THEME: _____
(copied from sandbox)

→ Brainstorm all the different things you could talk/write/blog/video about this month's theme. Get specific. The more specific, the better.

Put your ideas in the bucket. Refer back to often for inspiration.

WEEKLY PLAN...

Lets talk FREE STuff, shall we...

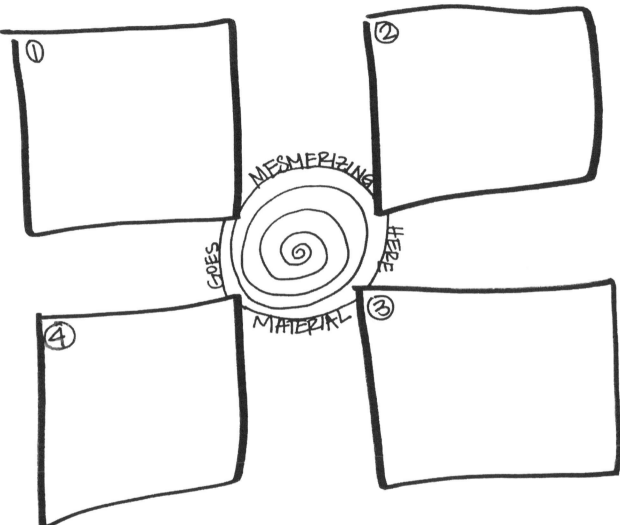

①

②

MESMERIZING

GOES   HERE

MATERIAL

④

③

...Everyone loves free stuff. It's what attracts people to your business. In each box above, choose a topic of the week that revolves around your theme of the month. HINT: Check your idea bucket.

→Write down what you will do to share that content with others.

    TIP: Free content are things like blog posts, infographics, lists, opt-ins, podcasts, videos, webinars, etc.

→Make the commitment and add them to your planner with due dates.

this month's December 2017

theme

reminders

goals

$ (drawn symbol)

sunday	monday	tuesday
3	4	5
10	11	12
17	18	19
24 / 31	25	26

things to get done this month

- Order Biz Plan Book 2017 Edition!
-
-
-
-
-

this month's newsletter(s)

mailing date(s):

topic:

related free content:

ways to generate buzz:

wednesday	thursday	friday	saturday
		1	2
	Order Biz Plan Book 2018 Edition!		
6	7	8	9
13	14	15	16
20	21	22	23
27	28	29	30

ideas | brainstorming | brilliance

December 2017

this week's focus	4 monday

good stuff	5 tuesday

	6 wednesday
"If you are feeling lost and find yourself wondering what somebody else would do, STOP! Wonder what YOU will do!" Stacy Galiczynski AlongCameLife.com	

email/newsletter/promo ideas

7 thursday

to-do's

3 most important tasks

1.

2.

3.

8 friday

9 saturday

10 sunday

ideas | brainstorming | brilliance

December 2017

this week's focus	⑪ monday
good stuff	⑫ tuesday
"Professionals have a plan B. Entrepreneurs have a plan C, D and keep going till something sticks." Yvette Sonneveld InboundMarketingBliss.com	⑬ wednesday

email/newsletter/promo ideas

14 thursday

to-do's

3 most important tasks

1.

2.

3.

15 friday

16 saturday   **17** sunday

ideas | brainstorming | brilliance

December 2017

this week's focus	**18** monday

good stuff	**19** tuesday

| "Within your community, inspire each other to achieve things that you never thought possible. Beyond that circle, sacrifice, serve, support." Warren Henderson | **20** wednesday |

email/newsletter/promo ideas

21 thursday

22 friday

23 saturday

24 sunday

to-do's

3 most important tasks

1.
2.
3.

ideas | brainstorming | brilliance

December 2017

this week's focus

25 monday

good stuff

26 tuesday

"How you spend your moments, is how you spend your life."

Felicia Slattery
FeliciaSlattery.com

27 wednesday

email/newsletter/promo ideas

28 thursday

to-do's

3 most important tasks

1.

2.

3.

29 friday

30 saturday   **31** sunday

ideas | brainstorming | brilliance

Monthly Checkin !

This is powerful stuff! ➤

"It is only in the review of your performance that you can have breakthroughs." -Steven Griffith

IMPORTANT: At the end of every month, take the time to reflect on how you felt about the past month, what you accomplished and what you feel you could improve on in the upcoming month.

➤ From 1-10, how do you feel about the past month?

➤ What was your favorite thing that happened this past month. Describe it:

_____

_____

_____

_____

➤ What are the three biggest lessons you learned from the past month?

_____

_____

_____

_____

➤ Review the past month of your PlanBook and assess your priorities. Did you accomplish what you set out to? Are you happy with your results and how you spent your time? If not, what steps can you take to improve in the upcoming month?

_____

_____

_____

_____

_____

_____

➤ What is one thing you accomplished this past month? What did you do to celebrate your accomplishment?

_____

_____

_____

_____

_____

➤ Do you feel that you are still in alignment with your goals? If not, explain why and what's changed for you in the past month.

_____

_____

_____

_____

_____

➤ Name three things you can improve on this upcoming month to keep you moving towards your goals. List concrete action steps you can take towards making these improvements.

_____

_____

_____

_____

_____

➤ Who or what are you especially grateful for from this past month? Describe in detail your gratitude and how it makes you feel. If it's a person, what is a way you can express your gratitude to them?

_____

_____

_____

_____

_____

Notes

Thoughts | Ideas | Brainstorming | Brilliance

Notes

Thoughts | Ideas | Brainstorming | Brilliance

Notes

Thoughts | Ideas | Brainstorming | Brilliance

Notes

Thoughts | Ideas | Brainstorming | Brilliance

Notes

Thoughts | Ideas | Brainstorming | Brilliance

Notes

Thoughts | Ideas | Brainstorming | Brilliance

Notes

Thoughts | Ideas | Brainstorming | Brilliance

Thoughts | Ideas | Brainstorming | Brilliance

Notes

Thoughts | Ideas | Brainstorming | Brilliance

Notes

Thoughts | Ideas | Brainstorming | Brilliance

Notes

Thoughts | Ideas | Brainstorming | Brilliance

Notes

Thoughts | Ideas | Brainstorming | Brilliance

Notes

Thoughts | Ideas | Brainstorming | Brilliance

Notes

Thoughts | Ideas | Brainstorming | Brilliance

_____
_____
_____
_____
_____
_____
_____
_____
_____
_____
_____
_____
_____
_____
_____
_____
_____
_____
_____
_____
_____
_____
_____
_____

Don't Forget!

Order Your 2018 Biz Plan Book Today!

Available on Amazon.com!
(In the 4th quarter of 2018)

62827736R00134

Made in the USA
Charleston, SC
21 October 2016